THE
SHEPHERD
AND HIS STAFF

A Guide to the Biblical Principles and Practices of Leadership

THEODORE MISTRA

In the Bible the shepherd's staff appears as a source of comfort, concern and compassion, often symbolizing the Spirit of God. In Moses' hand, it was a sign of God's miracles and deliverance. It parted seas. To David, the Lord's rod and staff were a source of comfort. The staff had a type of aura about it. Shepherds used a variety of equipment and aids while tending their flocks, but the staff was mainly practical, used by shepherds to draw sheep together, guide them, rescue them and set them free from entanglement.

In *The Shepherd and His Staff*, our examples of the qualities of a good shepherd and the uses of his staff start with Abraham, then cover Moses and David, concentrating on the men called by God and their use of an actual wooden staff. When we move to Jesus and his 12 apostles we move from a wooden staff to human staffs. Jesus tells Peter to be a shepherd and to feed his flock. We end with those of us today who are heirs of Jesus as modern shepherds, and while we do not use a wooden staff we surround ourselves with human staffs just like Jesus did. It is no accident that the word *shepherd* has the words "she" and "he" in it. As women and men serving in his Kingdom we are **living staffs** used by the Lord to guide and lead his sheep as he would have. This book illustrates the key characteristics a living staff should have, as we also lead as good shepherds.

The Shepherd and His Staff: A Guide to the Biblical Principles and Practices of Leadership

Copyright ©2017 Theodore Mistra
1st edition 2004, 2nd Edition 2005, 3rd Edition 2008, 4th Edition 2017
Previous ISBN 1-58597-303-3 Leathers Publishing
All rights reserved
Printed in Canada and the United States of America
ISBN 978-1-927355-93-0 soft cover
ISBN 978-1-927355-94-7 EPUB

Published by:
Castle Quay Books
Burlington, Ontario
In the USA
Lake Worth, Florida
Tel: (416) 573-3249
E-mail: info@castlequaybooks.com   www.castlequaybooks.com

Cover and inside design by Burst Impressions
Printed at Essence Printing, Belleville, Ontario

Library and Archives Canada Cataloguing in Publication

Mistra, Theodore, author
    The shepherd and his staff : a guide to the biblical principles and practices of leadership / Theodore Mistra.

Previously published: Leathers Publishing, 2004.
Issued in print and electronic formats.
ISBN 978-1-927355-93-0 (softcover).--ISBN 978-1-927355-94-7 (EPUB)

    1. Leadership--Religious aspects--Christianity. I. Title.

BV4597.53.L43M57 2017   248.8'8   C2017-905261-6
                                                 C2017-905262-4

CASTLE QUAY BOOKS

For my father, who served as a lieutenant colonel in the United States Army, in memoriam. And for our Father in heaven and Jesus his Son, who sent the Holy Spirit to inspire full appreciation of my father's true legacy.

Contents

Foreword by Ken Blanchard

The headlines of the world's newspapers report daily on the growing evidences of man's inhumanity to man. CNN.com, under all its headings—U.S., World, Money, Opinion, Health, Sports, Politics, Tech, Entertainment, Travel, and Style—conveys that relationships in each field are in deep trouble. Even the most ostrich-like of us becomes aware that if realizations are not made and actions immediately taken in light of the intrinsic connectedness of the human family, we will not even save the earth, let alone establish the Kingdom of God on it.

Paralleling this process of destruction, however, is another process not so well advertised, focused on or debated. It is characterized by a growth of consciousness that "winning," if somebody else has to lose, doesn't "taste" right. Indeed it has the effect of turning the sweetness to sawdust in the mouth. A growing number of people are daring to believe that "win/win" might be a possibility; that life is not about "either/or" but instead is about "both/and." And with that realization there is an experience of relief at the level of the soul.

Onto such a stage comes *The Shepherd and His Staff: A Guide to Leadership*. While the author is completely honest that the source of his inspiration is his own spiritual heritage of a personal relationship with Jesus Christ, he states, "The principles and practices are intended to benefit Christian, Jew and Muslim alike."

Such a statement, so genuinely expressed, lifts the book to a new level. The interest is in serving a community that includes Christianity and reaches out to include all the dwellers of the earth. As such, it is a beautiful expression of the spirit of Christ himself.

For those who are interested in widening their horizons to include the entire human family, the spirit and advice of this book will assist them in developing transformative behaviors. It will also serve as a balm to the heart.

Ken Blanchard
Scotland

Foreword by Blaine McCormick

Make no mistake, servant leadership was a great idea and remains a great idea in the twenty-first century. Robert K. Greenleaf's reflections on the nature of power and authority in a competitive world are as vibrant and challenging today as they were when they emerged in the early 1970s. Greenleaf spent much of his life in the business arena working for AT&T and was no stranger to the realities of organizational life. Later, he witnessed the cultural upheavals of the sixties and seventies and concluded that our thinking on leadership was deeply flawed. His ideas about servant leadership have stood the test of both time and practice. As a business professor, it gives me great pride to say that an idea of tremendous spiritual depth emerged from a businessman reflecting on his life and work. Maybe we underestimate the spiritual depths that can be plumbed by those of us who live and work in the marketplace.

Three decades later, another deeply spiritual model of leadership is emerging. More interesting, it appears that God is once again using businesspeople to bring a new way of thinking about leadership into the marketplace of ideas. This time, however, the vision is spread among a variety of people in a variety of locations.

In 1992, I left corporate America to enter the academic world. A little more than a decade later, after years of meditating on Psalm 23 as a leadership text, I co-authored a book titled *Shepherd Leadership*. Not long after this book hit the shelf, I learned that at least two other businesspeople had put pen to paper to clarify what it means to be a shepherd leader. Theodore Mistra is one of these people.

In this book, Mistra combines many years of business life and deep reflection to tell us what it means to be a shepherd leader. Not confining himself to only one psalm, he confidently guides the reader through the entire Bible. Time and time again, he shows that our world and decision set are much broader than we think them to be.

Beyond this, he demonstrates by example the importance of caring for those on our path who need it most. Guiding us down new paths, creating for us a larger world, caring for us—that's what shepherds do, and that's what Mistra has done with his life.

It shouldn't surprise us that businesspeople are capable of such spiritual insight. After all, God used an accountant to write the first book of the New Testament. And that King David fellow who wrote all of those psalms? Well, he grew up working the family business: shepherding. This book is evidence that the Spirit of God still moves in the marketplace.

Blaine McCormick
Co-author, *Shepherd Leadership*
Baylor University

Introduction

The Transformation of a Leader

Over 30 years ago, I was the executive vice president and chief financial officer of a small company. My background included an MBA from one of the top business schools in the world, significant management experience in Fortune 500 companies and a very ambitious Type A personality, all under the banner of being a Christian. How I ended up at a small company is another story for another time.

Shortly after I joined the company, we decided to leverage our assets and invest a significant amount of money to enter a new market. Because the company had negative net worth, the bank required both the president and me to personally guarantee a loan in order to fund the investment. This was not a problem for me because I was convicted that God had called me to this company and that God's hand was on me and on the future of the company. As a matter of fact, I strongly believed that I was on a mission for his glory, and this conviction is what sustained me through this turnaround.

By the grace of God and hard work, we successfully entered the new market. Within a year or so, the company turned the corner and became profitable. I believed we were on a roll and that God would continue to bless us and there would be no harm. The company even negotiated an attractive health insurance premium from our group provider, which lowered our costs and added to our profitability. What could go wrong?

Shortly after this financial turnaround, one of our supervisors approached me with information about a new hire. He was an entry level employee who was actually very sick and needed major heart surgery. I immediately thought that we would face unexpected catastrophic medical costs, the group premium would increase and the company's financial recovery would be in jeopardy. I was angry with the supervisor for hiring him. I was angry with the employee, who I thought knew he was sick and just wanted a job for health insurance benefits. In short, I believed he was trying to take advantage of us. My initial reaction was to find an excuse to terminate him, but something unexplainable in human terms caused me to pause.

As a Christian I knew I wanted to make the right decision, but I also struggled with how the world makes decisions, and that was just too easy. There had to be a better way. What did God want me to do? Did God want me to sacrifice one employee for the good of the company? Frankly, I was paralyzed about making a decision. I didn't know what to do.

Finally, my wife suggested we go for a weekend drive so I could think clearly. Along the way, my frustration grew, until finally, gripping the steering wheel, I loudly called out to God for help. "What do you want me to do? You called me to this company, gave us financial success, and now it could be taken away. Do you really want to jeopardize the other staff for the sake of this one person?"

Then in a calm and deliberate voice my wife responded, "You are a shepherd to your employees. What would a shepherd do?"

I was thunderstruck. So simple an answer, yet so powerful! A rush descended from my head down to my feet, and a huge burden lifted off my shoulders. I knew God had spoken to me through my wife. I had my answer, and I was going to be obedient in his eyes, not the eyes of the world.

The next day, I went to the employee and told him not to worry and to get better soon because we wanted him back. The company would support him. He turned to me and said, "Don't you worry. The hospital is performing the surgery for free, and all related expenses are being covered by them."

To this day, I dread to consider what would have happened if I had not listened and surrendered to God's will to take care of this single needy, lonely and suffering individual. What a lesson to learn! It was not only about profits but about people. About the people God puts under our care. It's a lesson so easily forgotten in today's business environment, where we hear time and time again that success is measured by financial achievement.

As businesspeople, our roles are played out in the context of various relationships—with God, our families, board members, senior executives, employees, clients or customers, vendors, shareholders and others. Interactions occur at every level of leadership as well, whether in personal, one-on-one, team or organizational realms. The same can be said of our roles at home and in every aspect of life. As the story of my dilemma and decision illustrates, conflicts in business often arise in the midst of competing priorities.

For many, the Bible, a source of truth and wisdom, provides the foundation for a consistent approach to leadership. Thus began my lifelong journey to study the Scriptures and transform my leadership style, including transforming my mind, heart and soul to learn what a shepherd would do. It is a journey I have been on for over 20 years that continues to transform me in ways I would have never thought possible, but God knew.

This book is about leadership. It is, in fact, about the greatest leader who ever lived. In *The Servant Leader: Transforming Your Heart, Head, Hands, and Habits*, Ken Blanchard and Phil Hodges encourage us to follow Jesus as the ultimate example of leadership for all purposes. As such, what he demonstrated as a relevant leadership model is to be a shepherd. I have learned that an executive's highest calling is to become a shepherd leader.

The purpose of this book is to encourage you—through the sharing of experiences, insights, and reflections—to become like a shepherd in your business and personal life settings. While inspired by my spiritual heritage of a personal relationship with Jesus Christ, the principles and practices are intended to benefit Christian, Jew and Muslim alike. As a matter of fact, the message is all-inclusive, extending to people of all faiths in all societies. My heart's desire—and the intent of this book—is for you to receive spiritual nourishment while developing the head, heart, hands and habits of a shepherd.

A series of key questions will arise in the process of encouraging you to recognize and respond to your high calling to lead like Jesus and be a good shepherd. If Jesus, as a shepherd, is the ultimate leadership model for all purposes, how did he really lead? What wisdom did he impart to those closest to him? Why is shepherd leadership a more relevant model than traditional business school teaching and conventional wisdom?

Management theories and practices abound. Some have proven valuable, a few extraordinarily so. Several have been passing fancies. In any event, the list of possibilities is endless. Bookshelves in stores, libraries and personal collections sag under the weight of the subject.

From the early days of 1920s experiments regarding organizational development, focusing on human relations and motivation, through Drucker's impressive body of work, to the latest leading edge research efforts, every conceivable approach to management has been considered.

In the midst of it all, what difference could shepherd leadership possibly make, and why does it matter? Who is called to be a shepherd, and what does any of this have to do with you or me? Finally, how does a leader answer the universal call to be a shepherd? What is the true character and nature of the leader as shepherd, and how does it apply in business and other arenas of life?

To help fulfill the purpose and intent of this guide, each issue will be considered in turn. Yet a simple and straightforward question appears at the threshold. Why look to the shepherd?

Jesus called himself one. He saw others as shepherds as well. God the Father spoke of both himself and his Son as shepherds. He also saw his chosen leaders as shepherds. From Abraham to Zephaniah, throughout the Old and New Testaments alike, the shepherd is present and prominent. In Islamic faith and culture, before becoming a prophet Muhammad grew up as a shepherd. In terms both literal and figurative, the shepherd is on the scene, whether caring for a modest flock near the smallest village or presiding as head of state for a vast nation.

In summary, the Bible reveals the shepherd as a leadership calling, role and responsibility with equal force for men and women. When reading about a "shepherd" in a leadership context, please remember that it applies to any person who has any power or influence over another person. The key precept is that this influence is to be used to glorify God, whether in the home, church, schools, business or government. The shepherd transcends time and place, eclipses economic and social status, and bridges the political spectrum. If Jesus, the ultimate role model for leadership, saw himself as and was seen as a shepherd, how did he in turn teach and train those closest to him?

Thank you, Jesus, for your unmerited favor in calling me to be a shepherd to your flock that you entrusted to my care.

Reflection: A Shepherd's Staff

Shepherds use a variety of equipment and aids while tending their flocks. Items commonly or occasionally used include a rod, staff (also referred to as a scepter), sling (like the one used by David to slay Goliath), bag or pouch, garments, a tent, dogs, and a watch-tower.

In the Bible and throughout literature, the staff appears as a source of comfort, concern and compassion, often symbolizing the Spirit of God. In Moses' hand, it was a sign of God's miracles and deliverance. Of course, the staff was mainly of practical use by shepherds to draw sheep together, guide them, rescue them and set them free from entanglement.

A staff holds special significance for me. In our company, I try to move through the facilities on twice daily "walkabouts," a way to keep a finger on the pulse of the workplace and show concern for our people. Far from rote, it has become a special time to connect with others each day, and I cherish the moments.

One day, in the midst of a room filled with a few dozen workers, I noticed an employee whose demeanor seemed downcast. I found out that she had contemplated suicide over the previous weekend and began acting in an unusual fashion. After careful consideration, the human resources manager and I conducted an intervention and took her to an emergency room. Our intent was to leave her in the care of medical professionals.

It was not to be. With a crowd in the ER and a waiting time sure to stretch for several hours, we sat alongside her, not wanting to leave her alone. The time together gave us a chance for a dialogue. As we talked, the floodgates opened. We heard one story after another of physical and verbal abuse she had experienced, which combined to shatter any sense of worth and to instill a sense of utter desperation in her. We listened and, with compassion, shared the unconditional nature of God's love for each of us.

After returning home from the hospital that night, she grew convinced that God loved her and would not forsake her, because, even though she was hiding her face, we had seen her in a crowded setting. The next day, she was back at work with a smile on her face, ready to begin the long road to recovery. She shared how her burden was lifting and thanked and hugged us for caring enough about her to reach out.

A few days later, my wife and I were on a trip on our twenty-fifth wedding anniversary. We happened upon an antique shop. I entered and quickly moved to the back of the store, but my wife lingered near the entrance. Inside the front door, she spotted a shepherd's staff, the first either of us had ever seen. She knew it was for me, representing a tangible confirmation of my role as a shepherd in the workplace. With God's hand in all things, we returned home with the staff in hand.

The next morning during my daily devotion, I opened my journal to record our experience. As I glanced down, I noticed the last Scripture verse I noted before leaving on our trip: "Shepherd your people with your staff, the flock of your inheritance" (Mic. 7:14).

The shepherd's staff now hangs in my office. It serves as a daily reminder to be a leader like Jesus, whose righteousness is the scepter of his kingdom (Ps. 45:6; Heb. 1:8).

The Original Peter Principle

The Peter Principle is a theory that originated in a 1969 book by the same name (Peter is the author's last name). The principle is based on the notion that every employee in a hierarchy tends to rise to the level of his own incompetence. It addresses in a lighthearted but pointed way why things seem to go wrong in the workplace.

The Peter Principle has demonstrated some utility over the years. But there's another version infinitely more important. It's one that dates back 2,000 years or so, and it was coined by Jesus himself in his final instructions to Peter the Apostle.

The inner circle of women and men who followed Jesus was an amazingly diverse group despite shared circumstances. His disciples all had vastly different personalities. They also spanned the political spectrum. One was from a radical group determined to overthrow the existing civil government. But another was a tax collector in collusion with the existing government and essentially a traitor to his own people.

Professionally, at least four of the twelve disciples, and possibly seven, were fishermen and close friends from the same town. They probably knew each other since childhood. The others were likely tradesmen or craftsmen, but we are not told what they did before leaving everything to become followers of Christ. Most of them were from Galilee, an agricultural region at the intersection of trade routes. Jesus himself was a carpenter from a family of carpenters.

Many women were on the scene as part of Jesus' core group as well. They were with him all the way from Galilee to Jerusalem. They were close by when he was crucified. In the end, women were the first people he visited after the resurrection.

Behind Jesus, however, one individual stood as leader of the pack. Peter led a core team of three (including John and James) as well as the overall group. He always seemed to be front and center and typically acted as spokesman. Jesus chose Peter, as the first among equals, for a special leadership role and then shaped him during their years together. According to theological dictionaries, the word translated as "first" in Matthew 10:2—"first, Simon (who is called Peter)"—is actually the Greek term *protos*. The reference signifies the first in rank or the chief. Peter embodies how the Lord authors a leader among leaders.

At the end of his time on earth, after a miraculous catch of fish from the Sea of Tiberias, Jesus provided Peter with the ultimate marching orders for leadership purposes. Despite Peter's intense fishing background and the disciples' initial call to become "fishers of men," Jesus used a different model—a shepherd. John, another key leader even closer to Jesus than Peter was, provided an eyewitness account.

After three years of intensive leadership teaching and training, when Jesus entrusted Peter with his final encouragement and instructions, it all came down to one thing. He repeated the message so there could be no mistake—"Feed my lambs." "Take care of my sheep." "Feed my sheep." In the end, the original Peter Principle is to "be a shepherd."

Jesus concluded with the exhortation "Follow me!" It was precisely the same call he issued to Peter by the Sea of Galilee at the outset. In other words, Jesus brought Peter full circle while making him a leader in his own image. The rugged fisherman had been transformed into a shepherd. He was also sent off to teach other leaders how to be shepherds and transform the world.

Jesus used the shepherd concept two millennia ago to cut across professional, economic, political and social boundaries at personal, one-on-one and group levels. The shepherd concept, however, was not limited to Jesus and his relationship with Peter. Nor was it confined to a particular time, place or circumstance.

From the beginning, God has used and allowed a series of approaches to the administration, leadership and management of people and their affairs. The historical sequence ranges from direct relationship with human beings to a series of intermediate organizational structures, involving, at various biblical times, priests, prophets, judges and kings. Sometimes God initiated his own plan, and sometimes he responded to the passionate desires and relentless appeals of his people.

Modern counterparts also include monarchies and extend from democracies to dictatorships, with everything (or nothing) in between. In each instance, there have been both good and bad examples of a given form of governance and of the people who serve as leaders within it. Unfortunately, all too often the examples have been negative.

Regardless of environment, the shepherd concept is a common denominator, appearing as a current running beneath the course of history. After the exodus from Egypt, Moses (a shepherd), on the advice of Jethro (whose daughters were shepherds), organized his nation into groups and a structure of units over which individuals called judges were placed. Judges served as principal leaders of the people from the time of Joshua's death to the reign of Saul, Israel's first king. David, the shepherd king who was a man after God's own heart, succeeded Saul.

Since the days of Abel, the son of Adam and Eve, the shepherd has been used in instrumental ways. The entire Bible is rich with illustrations. Abraham, Rachel, Joseph, Jethro's daughters, Moses, Midian's daughters and David were all shepherds. Even Jesus himself is referred to as one.

The role of shepherd transcends time, place and circumstance. It also cuts across all styles of management, all types of organizational structures and systems, all positions of civil and religious authority and all cultural settings. God has always used leaders and considered them to be shepherds in every conceivable situation. He's using them now. And he always will.

Shepherd leadership, the original Peter Principle, is relevant at personal, one-on-one, team and organizational levels of leadership. In our current postmodern world, where technology and intellectual property drive business and industry, a shepherd is called to make a difference, to follow a new path to transforming the world.

Two Key Principles of Shepherd Leadership

God (the Father) has used the shepherd throughout history. He speaks of himself as a shepherd and sees people in leadership positions as shepherds. His shepherding perspective applies whether a given leader is in a position of public or private authority, in a rural or urban setting, or at the local or national level.

Jesus (the Son) was the ultimate role model for leadership. His consistent actions and explicit instructions were clear and compelling. He taught and trained Peter, his number-one protégé, and the rest of his closest followers to be like shepherds for leadership purposes. The shepherd model stems from two key principles: (1) be a good shepherd and (2) develop other shepherd leaders.

(1) Be a Good Shepherd

The first key principle is to be a good shepherd. A leader cannot adopt a leadership model; he must become one. The principle and process begin deep within the person. Becoming a shepherd involves starting at the heart level. The heart must be transformed into the very heart of the Great Shepherd. "And we all, who with unveiled faces contemplate the Lord's glory, are being transformed into his image with ever-increasing glory, which comes from the Lord, who is the Spirit" (2 Cor. 3:18).

Certain heart-level truth is clear from Jesus' life and leadership, his classic teachings on the subject and other relevant Scriptures.

- A leader knows and is known by his followers (from John 10, in which Jesus speaks about the shepherd and the flock).
- A leader looks after each and every one of his followers (from Luke 15, in which Jesus tells the parable of the lost sheep).

- A leader nourishes his followers (from John 21, in which Jesus encourages Peter to follow him in feeding and caring for others).

Ultimately, according to Jesus, a leader would lay down his life for his people (figuratively speaking, but meaningfully and practically as well).

The leadership principle of becoming a shepherd actually appears throughout the Old and New Testaments of the Bible. Certain passages in particular, like the thirty-fourth chapter of Ezekiel, are worthy of careful study. The comprehensive plan—to be a good shepherd—easily drawn from all of the relevant Scriptures may be summarized in simple and effective terms as follows.

To be a good shepherd involves relationships in two dimensions, providing crystal clear structure and direction. One dimension is our individual personal relationship with God. The other dimension extends to our relationships with each other.

At the threshold, each of us is called to a relationship of purpose and meaning with the Great Shepherd. We are to love God with all of our heart, mind, and soul. Only then is it truly possible to be transformed into a leader—a shepherd—after God's own heart. In turn, we are also able to begin loving others as we love ourselves.

RELATIONSHIPS

■ Vertical dimension—our personal relationship with God

- God is in command. He is like a sheepmaster, which is one who is both a shepherd and the owner of the sheep. God cares for his people like a shepherd tends the flock (Ezek. 34:30–31).
- God gathers people in his arms and carries them close to his heart. He gently leads those with young ones (Isa. 40:11).
- God wants his people to have leaders after his own heart, who lead with knowledge and understanding (Jer. 3:15).

■ Horizontal dimension—our relationships with each other

- According to Merriam-Webster's dictionary, a shepherd is one employed in tending, feeding, and guarding sheep in flocks. That's just the beginning, as far as God is concerned.
- God intends his chosen leaders (i.e., shepherds), in ways both literal and figurative, to

- Gather
- Account for
- Search for and look after
- Rescue
- Tend
- Feed
- Protect
- Provide rest for
- Care for
- Bind up the injured
- Strengthen the weak
- Judge
- Save
- Watch over the people for whom they are responsible (Ezek. 34:11-24).

The first key principle also provides clarity of measurement in terms of accountability and outcomes. In the end, the differences between a good shepherd and an irresponsible one—with consequences for everyone involved—become all too clear.

MEASUREMENTS

■ Accountability

- Leaders are expected to accomplish all that pleases God (Isa. 44:28).
- Leaders who lack understanding turn to their own way in search of personal gain (Isa. 56:11).
- God holds leaders accountable for their people, his flock (Ezek. 34:10).
- What leader can stand against God? (Jer. 49:19).

■ Outcomes

- The life of a flock (team, group, or organization) or any particular sheep (person) depends on the shepherd who leads it.
- If leaders honor God and serve his people, blessings, growth, peace, prosperity, safety and well-being will come (Ezek. 34:25-29).
- If leaders fail to honor God and serve his people, leaders will be shattered (Jer. 51:23). People will be scattered (Nah. 3:18; Zech. 10:2, 13:7).

Simply put, God calls leaders to be good shepherds.

(2) Develop Shepherd Leaders

The second key principle is to develop other shepherd leaders. To effectuate organizational mission and strategy, there is a need to perpetuate the leadership paradigm throughout the organization. It is also essential to plan for transition and prepare for leadership changes. Unless the leader multiplies his or her leadership and plans for succession, the vision of the leader will be limited and short-lived.

As God approaches leadership, he has a multiplication and succession plan in place. There's a clearly established line of shepherding responsibility and delegation of authority for all in a position of leadership. God the Father not only clearly speaks of himself being a shepherd and consistently acts as one; he embodies active development of his followers as shepherd leaders. A leading example is Moses, someone who actually—and amazingly—knew God on a face-to-face basis (Deut. 34:10).

Who was Moses? He was someone chosen by God to be—and he chose to become—a shepherd leader. Moses also was someone who chose to be identified with his own people, even to be mistreated with them, rather than to enjoy a life of comfort and privilege with his adoptive ruling family. In the process, he declined the treasures of Egypt, a great nation in its heyday, accepting instead temporary disgrace on earth while looking ahead to a more lasting reward.

Moses' résumé as a shepherd leader is remarkable:

- He led his people out of slavery and oppression in Egypt, risking the anger and retribution of the ruling authorities.
- He kept his people's Passover tradition, protecting innocent children and preserving entire generations in the process.
- He led his people through the Red Sea as on dry land, conquering their foes along the way.

How is Moses remembered? The Bible prominently records him as of one of the all-time heroes of faith (Heb. 11:23–29). It also says of him, "No one has ever shown the mighty power or performed the awesome deeds that Moses did" (Deut. 34:12).

As an additional dimension to his legacy, one of the most important things he ever accomplished was to develop another shepherd leader and choose a successor. The way in which he did so provides inspired guidance for leaders today. A blueprint for leadership development, multiplication and succession, as exemplified by Moses, may be drawn from Numbers 27. According to God's divine plan, the shepherd leader does the following:

- Hears from God (Num. 27:12–14)
- Prays and remains patient until God reveals a successor (Num. 27:15–17)
- Seeks and selects a successor filled with the Holy Spirit (Num. 27:18)
- Empowers (lays hands on) the successor (Num. 27:18)
- Presents the successor before the community (Num. 27:19)
- Delegates authority to the successor (Num. 27:20)
- Inaugurates and commissions the successor as instructed by God (Num. 27:21–23)
- Continues to walk with God until the end, accepting God's peace about the successor (Deut. 34:1–6)

What were the outcomes? How did it turn out for Moses, the shepherd, Joshua, his successor, and their people? His people were in the right hands—God's and those of a shepherd leader. Personally, he enjoyed a long life with clear faculties and continued strength up until the end and the sure knowledge of a proper successor. The short- and long-term results for all concerned are worthy of note (Deut. 34):

- Moses was a hundred and twenty years old when he died, yet his eyes were not weak, nor was his strength gone (v. 7).
- People wept and mourned for him after his death (v. 7–8).
- Joshua was filled with wisdom because Moses followed God's divine plan for choosing a successor (v. 9).
- The people listened to Joshua and followed God (v. 9).

In addition, God's divine plan for leadership multiplication and succession was demonstrated and recorded, remaining available for leaders today.

Moses must have been disappointed after coming close enough to see the Promised Land but not being able to enter it. After all he had accomplished and everything he had endured, it was a potentially bitter ending. Yet when he was asked to choose someone who would not only succeed him but also exceed him in the ability to enter into and enjoy the Promised Land, he did it. As all throughout his life, he was looking ahead to his ultimate reward.

Joshua in turn learned and followed well. Throughout his lifetime, the people served God. The leadership succession and multiplication plan also continued in place, as people remained true to God throughout the lifetimes of the elders who outlived Joshua. They had experienced firsthand the shepherd leadership of Joshua and witnessed all the great things the Lord had done for them. As leaders, they upheld the shepherd tradition (Josh. 24:28–33; Judg. 2:6–7).

Unfortunately, the next generation grew up not knowing God or what he had done for them. Leaders were shattered and people were scattered. As a result, God installed a line of judges in positions of leadership. Deborah, a great judge, stood apart as a vivid positive example. Fearless leadership and devotion to God's people rendered her blessed among women. She embodied a shepherd leader ready, willing and able to deliver and protect her people regardless of cost or risk.

At a later moment in history, God established a line of kings to supplant judges in leadership roles, beginning with Saul. Tragically, over time the number of kings who were bad shepherds, doing "evil in the eyes of the Lord," far exceeded those who were good shepherds, doing "what was right in the eyes of the Lord." The good shepherd tradition was largely broken for generation after generation. But not early on.

After Saul, God placed a true shepherd, David, as leader over his people. David in turn acknowledged God as his shepherd (Ps. 23:1) and was one himself, both literally (1 Sam.) and figuratively as the appointed king of one nation. Significantly, David was chosen not based on outward appearances or superficial criteria but based solely on matters of the heart (1 Sam. 16:7). He was, in fact, a man after God's own heart, the heart of a shepherd.

Moses and David have something in common besides being good shepherds. Just as Moses was unable to enter the Promised Land but chose a successor who did, David was unable to build the temple—one of his heart's desires—but was followed by a successor who did. David chose his son Solomon to inherit the throne. He charged him with final instructions before his death to be strong, walk in the Lord's ways at all times and show kindness when appropriate.

Solomon received unsurpassed wealth and authority as king. He asked for and received great wisdom. Unfortunately, through disobedience and refusal to act as a shepherd leader, he ultimately broke the shepherd tradition yet again. The principles of leaders as good shepherds and developing others as shepherds largely fell silent for ages. At least until the arrival of one appointed as Judge of all and King of kings.

Jesus came later as a shepherd. It was a role prophesied of him ("He will stand and shepherd his flock in the strength of the Lord, in the majesty of the name of the Lord his God" [Mic. 5:4]) and one he explicitly embraced ("I am the good shepherd" [John 10:11]). In the first chapter of Matthew, there's even a family tree that includes the genealogy from David to Jesus.

As heirs of Christ and his promises through faith, we stand directly in the line of succession as shepherds. The call to be a shepherd is as important and significant as any other call found in God's Word, whether to serve as priest or prophet, king or fisher of men. It also brings us full circle back to Jesus as the ultimate model for leadership and to the original Peter Principle: to be a good shepherd, just as Barnabas was when he brought Saul (who became Paul) to join the other apostles of Christ.

The bottom line is that we all are called to become a shepherd and develop other shepherds. So the key questions are, How does a leader answer the universal call to be a shepherd? What is the true character and nature of the leader as shepherd? How do we "be a shepherd" and develop others as shepherds? The essence of leaders as shepherds is found in their character, the sum of their thoughts, decision-making, words and actions. It exists in the substance of their heads, hearts, hands and habits.

Reflection: Our Chief Shepherd

The final encouragement and leadership teaching from Jesus to Peter must have made a lasting impression. Peter was a hard-core fisherman whom Jesus first called into a personal relationship with the appeal to become a "fisher of men." Later, when Peter wrote to Christians throughout the world, it would have been natural to use a metaphor from the realm of angling.

Did he? Hardly. The leader of Jesus' core group, known as The Rock, chose another distinctive word picture as the bedrock for his written legacy.

> For "you were like sheep going astray," but now you have returned to the Shepherd and Overseer of your souls. (1 Pet. 2:25)

> Be shepherds of God's flock that is under your care, watching over them —not because you must, but because you are willing, as God wants you to be; not pursuing dishonest gain, but eager to serve; not lording it over those entrusted to you, but being examples to the flock. And when the Chief Shepherd appears, you will receive the crown of glory that will never fade away. (1 Pet. 5:2-4)

In the process, Peter addresses two critical questions every leader must face at the personal leadership level. The first deals with your relationship with Christ and what level of control he will have in your life. Are you going to be a shepherd leader? Peter points us to one figure, the Shepherd and Overseer of our souls in the present tense, the Chief Shepherd at the end of days. The second deals with your life purpose. Are you going to develop other shepherd leaders? To follow in Jesus' footsteps, we are to become a shepherd to those under our care.

The Essence and Attributes of the Shepherd

Beyond the two key principles, a simple but effective acrostic has emerged over the years as a way to learn and teach the qualities of shepherd leadership. Overall, the essence of being a shepherd leader is a matter of significant depth, multiple dimensions and ongoing development. In the process of defining and describing what it means to be one, several key attributes have arisen:

S	Stewardship and Service
H	Hope and Humility
E	Example and Excellence
P	Perseverance and Prayer
H	Healing and Hearing
E	Encouragement and Endurance
R	Respect and Reconciliation
D	Decision and Discipline

What follows is a series of Scriptures, stories and insights corresponding to each attribute, as well as additional characteristics, compiled during the course of receiving and sharing the shepherd message over the years.

The Lord Is My Shepherd

Psalm 23, a psalm of David, portrays the Lord as both a compassionate caregiver and a fierce protector. Relevant verses follow that show part of the essence and attributes of the leader as shepherd.

The Lord Is My Water Buffalo Herder

American business culture measures success almost exclusively in financial terms. God measures success differently, by obedience and faith and how well his people are blessed and transformed under his chosen leadership. In April 2000, I was called to a matter of obedience and faith.

A business delegation was organized to visit Vietnam, and I was asked to teach a session on business basics. Through an interpreter, I made a "safe" presentation about certain principles and practices, including a description of an experience in overcoming an adverse situation after several years of heady success. Consistent with a prior agreement, and to avoid precipitating a political crisis, no mention was made of Jesus Christ.

One true test of leadership is how it handles adversity. The message seemed to resonate with an audience whose country experienced tragic turmoil and struggled to recover. Emboldened, I continued to communicate on the subject of management values and philosophies. Initially I wrote individual leadership characteristics on a flip chart. For ease of understanding, I summarized with the word "shepherd." Suddenly, however, people seemed puzzled, and the interpreter was aghast.

In the audience was a Vietnamese man who had lived in the United States and studied at an American university. He rescued the situation, and me, when he rose to translate. Finally, everyone began to nod their heads and relax. References to a shepherd were foreign to the listeners. He explained, however, how a shepherd has the same characteristics as the herdsman of water buffalo in Vietnam!

The message was delivered and accepted gratefully as we seemed to find common ground, not only with our mutual business experience but also on a deeper level about the essence of leadership. Despite cultural differences, individuals understood the role of a herdsman and the simple yet effective example of a shepherd. Barriers between us fell away, and I sensed we had bonded with them.

Later we attended a private reception with several dignitaries. As we were introduced, I was still uncertain of my presentation and whether a bond had indeed been established. To the glory of God, we were presented as businesspeople who exhibited the highest level of integrity...and as *Christians*.

SHEPHERD

Stewardship

> "Keep watch over yourselves and all the flock of which the Holy Spirit has made you overseers. Be shepherds of the church of God, which he bought with his own blood." (Acts 20:28)

STEWARDSHIP IN THE FACE OF ADVERSITY

Hanoi School of Business, Vietnam's equivalent of The Wharton School, sponsored the presentation I made to a group of university students and business leaders. The case study communicated was a story of stewardship resources and, more important, people. Afterward, the Vietnamese audience was eager to go beyond superficial matters, to learn more about leadership issues and insights. Their interest led to an in-depth discussion of the shepherd—or water buffalo herder—as a leadership model.

Here's the business case, which illustrates how a true test of leadership comes through adversity. After several years of growth on a heady 45-degree sales trajectory, the company enjoyed annual revenues of several million dollars with net profit margins in excess of 20 percent. The company also grew complacent and comfortable. Meanwhile, its largest single client accounted for 40 percent of revenues and 70 percent of profitability.

One morning, the company CEO had completed his exercise routine and was feeling relaxed and ready to head for the office when the telephone rang. The principal client called to give notice that they were terminating the business relationship. In a professional and succinct fashion, the client representative simply stated, "We really appreciate all of the work your company has done for us. We've now decided to bring the services in house."

In an instant, the CEO's mind flashed from human panic and anger to a Spirit-inspired response. "We really appreciate having your business for the past six years. Thank you. We'll do everything to make the transition as seamless and smooth as possible." He frankly did not know where the words came from because they belied his true feelings. Though he was fearful, an overwhelming calmness settled in as the words spontaneously came. Both the client and the CEO were surprised and relieved, the CEO because he spoke contrary to his first fleshly instinct, and the client for not having to face an onslaught of challenges and questions.

Panic returned when the CEO arrived at the office. Over time, however, several ingredients combined to create a turnaround for which God deserves the credit. Due to their previous stewardship of resources, there were enough cash reserves to weather the storm for eighteen months. With full shareholder support, the cash was invested in a concerted effort to rebuild the client base.

While the CEO wanted to terminate staff, the company president prevailed with another plan. There would be no layoffs. The company had the resources and a staff committed to weathering the crisis. They accepted the challenge. The experience was truly humbling for the CEO.

The following year sales fell by 25 percent, but the company managed to remain profitable through the prudent management of resources. The only departures of people came through natural attrition, so morale remained good. Exactly eighteen months after they lost the big client, revenues and profits were fully restored to the higher levels.

The leaders involved remain humbled by God's sovereign hand in the midst of adversity, leading them to steward his people and resources. At a personal level, the CEO will always remember God's grace in teaching him the importance of prayer, patience and passage of time—rather than impulsivity—in the role of steward and shepherd. Together, people throughout the company learned how a genuine sense of and commitment to culture and values are important to the health and success of an organization and the individuals within it— whether in good times or bad.

Service

SERVING GOD AND HIS FLOCK

Matt loved God. He also loved people, especially his wife and their four children. The man had true passion. And he was a true shepherd in the workplace, one who embodied his employer's culture and values in service to humanity.

Whether serving the interests of company clients or those of his co-workers, Matt, a follower of Jesus, led and treated others like a shepherd would. As a medical technologist and supervisor of a night shift, he, with his staff, processed and tested thousands of specimens each night. We all slept peacefully knowing Matt was on the job.

Matt was as relentless in caring for his team as he was in getting the work done right. Every Wednesday, he would joyfully provide everyone with food from the Joy Luck Chinese restaurant. He possessed a good sense of humor, and his laughter infected the workplace. If someone wished to speak with him on a personal topic, he'd take off his company ID badge, set it aside, put on his pastoral role and say, "Now, let's talk."

Matt was always on the lookout for answered prayer. The last time I was with him in the hospital, he was fighting a courageous battle with cancer and his vision was blurred. He asked me to read to him from his favorite book and chapter of the Bible. Somehow, the book in my lap already lay open to the exact page.

From Luke 10:27, I read Jesus' response to the question, what must be done to inherit eternal life? "'Love the Lord your God with all your heart and with all your soul and with all your strength and with all your mind'; and, 'Love your neighbor as yourself.'" For Matt, a genuine servant leader, it was an autobiography of his life and work. Matt died in the flesh from cancer, but his spirit and soul are alive because he inherited eternal life with God, his Father in heaven. His legacy as a shepherd in service to humanity lives on as well.

> What does the Lord your God ask of you but to fear the Lord your God, to walk in obedience to him, to love him, to serve the Lord your God with all your heart and with all your soul...? (Deut. 10:12)

> "Choose for yourselves this day whom you will serve." (Josh. 24:15)

"Worship the Lord your God, and serve him only." (Matt. 4:10)

"Whoever wants to become great among you must be your servant...just as the Son of Man did not come to be served, but to serve." (Matt. 20:26, 28)

Safety

————

The Lord Is My Shepherd

Even though I walk through the darkest valley, I will fear no evil, for you are with me; your rod and your staff, they comfort me. (Ps. 23:4)

————

SAFETY AND SECURITY: "But he brought his people out like a flock; he led them like sheep through the desert. He guided them safely, so they were unafraid; but the sea engulfed their enemies" (Ps. 78:52–53).

SEEK THE HOLY SPIRIT: "The righteous cry out, and the Lord hears them; he delivers them from all their troubles" (Ps. 34:17).

SPIRIT LED: "Teach me to do your will, for you are my God; may your good Spirit lead me on level ground" (Ps. 143:10).

STUDY SCRIPTURE: "All Scripture is God-breathed and is useful for teaching, rebuking, correcting and training in righteousness, so that the servant of God may be thoroughly equipped for every good work" (2 Tim. 3:16–17).

STAND FIRM AGAINST ADVERSITY: "Therefore put on the full armor of God, so that when the day of evil comes, you may be able to stand your ground, and after you have done everything, to stand" (Eph. 6:13).

Strength

He will stand and shepherd his flock in the strength of the Lord, in the majesty of the name of the Lord his God. (Mic. 5:4)

The name of the Lord is a fortified tower; the righteous run to it and are safe. (Prov. 18:10)

Salvation

THE SHEPHERDS' FIELD AND THE SAVIOR

Bethlehem is known as the town of David, the Shepherd King of Israel. On the outskirts, about a mile to the east, is a place called the Shepherds' Field. There's a story behind the name.

> And there were shepherds living out in the fields nearby, keeping watch over their flocks at night. An angel of the Lord appeared to them, and the glory of the Lord shone around them, and they were terrified. But the angel said to them, "Do not be afraid. I bring you good news that will cause great joy for all the people. Today in the town of David a Savior has been born to you; he is the Messiah, the Lord. This will be a sign to you: You will find a baby wrapped in cloths and lying in a manger."

> Suddenly a great company of the heavenly host appeared with the angel, praising God and saying, "Glory to God in the highest heaven, and on earth peace to those on whom his favor rests." When the angels had left them and gone into heaven, the shepherds said to one another, "Let's go to Bethlehem and see this thing that has happened, which the Lord has told us about."

> So they hurried off and found Mary and Joseph, and the baby, who was lying in the manger. When they had seen him, they spread the word concerning what had been told them about this child, and all who heard it were amazed at what the shepherds said to them. But Mary treasured up all these things and pondered them in her heart. The shepherds returned, glorifying and praising God for all the things they had heard and seen, which were just as they had been told. (Luke 2:8–20)

Leadership Insight

God calls us as shepherds to not focus on just the bottom line but to consider our role:

- **To steward the assets given to us to preserve and invest**
- **To serve those we are leading**
- **To provide a place of safety and security for our executives and employees**

As we consider this role and commit to it, we will find that our business is aligned with his purposes as we build it to grow and flourish.

SHEPHERD

Hope

It was after 5:00 p.m. on a bleak Friday in January. Paul, an executive, was slumped in his chair. A movement in the hallway snapped him to attention. Carolyn, the day supervisor, was standing at the door. Her presence seemed odd, since she finished each day at 1:00 p.m. Still absorbed in his own problems, Paul mechanically asked, "How are you doing?"

He barely listened as she confided that Donnie, her husband, had been diagnosed with fast-spreading terminal cancer. Given the best-case scenario—removal of most of his tongue and the left side of his face—Donnie declined treatment, feeling it was not worth it. Without hope for survival, he would live as best he could until the cancer took his life.

Empty of emotion, Paul's only response was "I'm sorry."

Home in bed less than twelve hours later, Paul was awakened by what seemed like an audible voice. "Get Donnie to M. D. Andersen in Houston!" Somewhat startled, he scanned the empty room, wondering who possibly could have given the instruction. With no one else present, he settled back to sleep, only to be roused again by the same voice and message.

At 6:00 a.m., Paul was on the phone with Carolyn's manager. By 8:00, they were speaking with Carolyn to tell her the message. She and Donnie had neither heard of M. D. Andersen Cancer Center, the top cancer hospital in the nation, nor been to Houston. Hardworking but humble people, they saw no hope for the necessary referrals and certainly had no resources to make a trip. Satisfied with his role as messenger, Paul felt his duty was fulfilled. It was for Carolyn and Donnie to figure out the details if they were interested.

Spontaneously, and surprising himself as much as the others, Paul blurted out, "Don't worry, Carolyn; we'll pay all travel expenses."

Moved to action, Carolyn's manager picked up the telephone and cold-called M. D. Andersen. Despite it still being early Saturday morning, within minutes the physician in charge of the head-and-neck department was on the line. The type of cancer afflicting Donnie was his specialty. The doctor was also developing an innovative new radiation protocol that would not involve any surgery. Carolyn's manager was dumbstruck, having fully expected to encounter only a voicemail system over the weekend, not the department head with a particular focus on Donnie's affliction.

In the days to follow, after enduring a series of qualifying tests, Donnie agreed to participate in the experiments. The treatment was fairly brutal in its own right, but Donnie persevered. Facing doubts and fears whether Donnie would survive the summer, Paul and others joined to anoint him with oil and pray for healing.

Months later, in November, and against all odds, Donnie attended the company's annual Christmas party. Just as he did the next year, and the year after that...

A couple of years later, Paul was recounting Donnie's hopeful story. It was Carolyn's turn to be rendered speechless. She had no recollection of having told Paul about Donnie and his condition on the bleak and ultimately momentous January day.

If it was not Carolyn, Paul has often wondered, then who stood at the door when the hour seemed so hopeless?

Those who hope in the LORD will renew their strength. They will soar on wings like eagles; they will run and not grow weary, they will walk and not faint. (Isa. 40:31)

And now these three remain: faith, hope and love. (1 Cor. 13:13)

Yes, my soul, find rest in God; my hope comes from him. (Ps. 62:5)

I have put my hope in your word. (Ps. 119:74)

The LORD delights in those who fear him, who put their hope in his unfailing love. (Ps. 147:11)

Hope deferred makes the heart sick, but a longing fulfilled is a tree of life. (Prov. 13:12)

And hope does not put us to shame, because God's love has been poured out into our hearts through the Holy Spirit, who has been given to us. (Rom. 5:5)

Be joyful in hope, patient in affliction, faithful in prayer. (Rom. 12:12)

If only for this life we have hope in Christ, we are of all people most to be pitied. (1 Cor. 15:19)

The glorious riches of this mystery, which is Christ in you, the hope of glory. (Col. 1:27)

But since we belong to the day, let us be sober, putting on faith and love as a breastplate, and the hope of salvation as a helmet. (1 Thess. 5:8)

We have this hope as an anchor for the soul, firm and secure. (Heb. 6:19)

Now faith is confidence in what we hope for and assurance about what we do not see. (Heb. 11:1)

All who have this hope in him purify themselves, just as he is pure. (1 John 3:3)

The Lord Is My Shepherd

Surely your goodness and love will follow me all the days of my life, and I will dwell in the house of the LORD forever. (Ps. 23:6)

Humility

Leaders as shepherds are to remain humble. All too often, leaders become self-serving and arrogant, believing in personal ownership and clinging to a sense of entitlement. To the contrary, the role of shepherd includes recognition that the flock belongs to God. Leaders are called to be humble stewards of a sacred trust as shepherds of God's flock and resources.

He has showed you, O mortal, what is good. And what does the Lord require of you? To act justly and to love mercy and to walk humbly with your God. (Mic. 6:8)

When pride comes, then comes disgrace, but with humility comes wisdom. (Prov. 11:2)

Wisdom's instruction is to fear the Lord, and humility comes before honor. (Prov. 15:33)

Do nothing out of selfish ambition or vain conceit. Rather, in humility value others above yourselves. (Phil. 2:3)

Be gentle toward everyone. (Titus 3:2)

All of you, clothe yourselves with humility toward one another, because, "God opposes the proud but gives grace to the humble." Humble yourselves, therefore, under God's mighty hand, that he may lift you up in due time. (1 Pet. 5:5–6)

HUMILITY AND HONESTY ARE THE BEST POLICY

The company had a new client with the potential for millions of dollars in revenue. Due to equipment problems beyond company control, the client ended up surprised and disappointed time and again. Every day for six weeks, the problem seemed to be solved. Yet just as soon as the client was given seemingly good news, another new problem would arise.

Finally, the client called to request a personal meeting. After a momentary feeling of fear, I recognized the meeting as an opportunity to provide a humble apology. Overruling staff objections, I decided to fully acknowledge our role in the problems and reinforce our sincere commitment to solve them.

When the meeting commenced, I said, "Before we begin, I apologize for any way in which the problems occurring in our company have disrupted the operations of your company. We take full responsibility. If there are any clients of yours you feel I should personally apologize to as well, I will do so right away."

With a smile on his face, the client looked at me and nodded. "All I wanted was to hear that you understood the impact the situation had on us. Only one thing I ask: in the future, if you have problems, please share them with us so we're not surprised and disappointed. Give us a regular update." That was it.

It was a valuable lesson in humility and honesty for our entire staff. Thank God for revealing the necessity of being a humble leader, providing a gracious client who could receive and accept a confession, and allowing us to move forward together in a new and revitalized relationship, one characterized by humility and honesty.

Honesty

An honest witness tells the truth. (Prov. 12:17)

Truthful lips endure forever. (Prov. 12:19)

Riches do not endure forever. (Prov. 27:24)

Leadership Insight

All employees go through periods of discouragement, whether it is about

- **Their personal life, which may be in chaos**
- **Their job: Is it worthwhile? Are they significant there?**
- **Their company: Is it stable? Will it succeed?**

It takes humility and honesty to portray the truth and then to speak hope that God will be our provider and leader. Each step is important as together we learn to follow him and let him be our hope.

SHEPHERD

Example

Be shepherds of God's flock that is under your care, watching over them—not because you must, but because you are willing, as God wants you to be; not pursuing dishonest gain, but eager to serve; not lording it over those entrusted to you, but being examples to the flock. (1 Pet. 5:2-3)

Excellence

IN SEARCH OF EXCELLENCE: THE SHEPHERD'S WAY

And David shepherded them with integrity of heart; with skillful hands he led them. (Ps. 78:72)

And yet I will show you the most excellent way. (1 Cor. 12:31)

But since you excel in everything—in faith, in speech, in knowledge, in complete earnestness and in the love we have kindled in you—see that you also excel in this grace of giving. (2 Cor. 8:7)

Whatever is true, whatever is noble, whatever is right, whatever is pure, whatever is lovely, whatever is admirable—if anything is excellent or praiseworthy—think about such things. (Phil. 4:8)

Those who have served well gain an excellent standing and great assurance in their faith in Christ Jesus. (1 Tim. 3:13)

And I want you to stress these things, so that those who have trusted in God may be careful to devote themselves to doing what is good. These things are excellent and profitable for everyone. (Titus 3:8)

MANUFACTURING EXCELLENCE, ONE DAY AT A TIME

Andrew was asked to lead a project involving service as a temporary CEO to a bankrupt manufacturing company. The company had run through $20 million in capital despite a wonderful high-technology healthcare product, solid patent protection and adequate distribution. Unable to manufacture enough product volume according to specification, the company tanked.

The first step taken was to start each day with prayer, asking God to show them how to fix the problem. Andrew was the first to arrive early each morning. As his team would gather, they would answer a few simple questions: What did we learn yesterday? How are we doing? What should we pursue next? Day by day, they were led to adjust one thing, learn from the results, and make another adjustment.

After sixty days, scrap product levels were reduced from 95 percent to 4 percent. In the process, the team transformed the company, which immediately became profitable. Leadership not only became excellent at manufacturing but excelled at—and served as an example of—seeking God, letting him provide direction, and responding with obedience.

> EXALT GOD: "Let them praise the name of the LORD, for his name alone is exalted" (Ps. 148:13).

> EDIFY ONE ANOTHER: "Let us therefore make every effort to do what leads to peace and to mutual edification" (Rom. 14:19).

Leadership Insight

As leaders, we are called to never ask anyone to do something we are not willing to demonstrate and live out for ourselves. As shepherds, we are always called to excellence—giving our best, paying attention, providing a product or service others can see as excellent—providing a platform for us to testify as to where excellence comes from. The source is the very nature of God in us, not to be found in just another activity or initiative.

SHEPHERD

Perseverance

PERSEVERANCE AND PLANTING SEEDS

By January, Simon had determined that the marketing effort at his company needed strong direction. When he thought of replacing certain staff members, God spoke to him and said, "They are my children. They hurt just like you hurt. Your role is not to lose them but to love them." Simon decided to be tough but fair.

They targeted a full range of potential client companies and began making sales calls, following up on each one of them. Over the next six months, they made more than three hundred sales presentations.

One night in mid-June, Simon woke up in a cold sweat. He was still new to the company, from another part of the country, and was hungry for Christian fellowship without knowing where to find it. Anxiety ridden, he looked up from bed to heaven (actually, toward the ceiling) and prayed, "Lord, I came here at your will and have done everything you asked. I've been diligent. When am I going to see some results?"

The next day he left on a business trip to call on three potential accounts. Between appointments, he visited a local Christian university, noticing its ornate yet modern architecture and sensing a great spirit among the students on campus. Then he encountered an exhibition facility in which was depicted various biblical themes. The multi-room exhibits culminated in a meditation room. While he sat along the wall, a taped message played across the fully carpeted, otherwise quiet room. The narrator spoke of "planting seeds." It was as if the Lord was answering his prayer from the night before.

In the first week of July, Simon's company signed their first client. Each following week brought new clients, until they began to come almost one every day. Simon began to fully understand the meaning of patience and perseverance, what it means to wait on the Lord. God was faithful, revealing his plan in season, not according to Simon's schedule. Through the summer and fall, company growth continued. Prayer was constant.

By November, the company had become aware of an opportunity to provide services for one of the largest companies in the world. Perhaps the Lord would reward them. Yet Simon was scared. They had sufficient energy and know-how but not enough resources.

The company made the sales pitch and won the account. Within a couple of months, they would need to renovate a facility, hire and train staff, design and implement a new computer system and assemble and then distribute a new product. It looked impossible, but God never let them down. Mistakes, rather than being fatal, became part of the learning process. Every day brought a new testimony of making it against all odds.

The company was ready in February, but just barely. Within another month, volume demands were burying operating capacity. The new six-figure computer system was unable to handle the work. The client considered pulling the account.

Simon was scared but kept his faith strong. The company negotiated hard and arranged for the design and creation of a parallel computer system at a cost also reaching six figures. Stepping out in faith, they made the investment. Within six weeks, the new system was in place and the business was saved. It had been another test of perseverance, one in which anxiety and worry decreased while seeds were being planted and faith was on the rise.

Therefore, since we are surrounded by such a great cloud of witnesses, let us throw off everything that hinders and the sin that so easily entangles. And let us run with perseverance the race marked out for us. (Heb. 12:1)

You need to persevere so that when you have done the will of God, you will receive what he has promised. (Heb. 10:36)

As you know, we count as blessed those who have persevered. You have heard of Job's perseverance and have seen what the Lord finally brought about. The Lord is full of compassion and mercy. (James 5:11)

Blessed is the one who perseveres under trial because, having stood the test, that person will receive the crown of life that the Lord has promised to those who love him. (James 1:12)

PLANTING SEEDS: "Do not be deceived: God cannot be mocked. A man reaps what he sows. Whoever sows to please their flesh, from the flesh will reap destruction; whoever sows to please the Spirit, from the Spirit will reap eternal life. Let us not become weary in doing good, for at the proper time we will reap a harvest if we do not give up" (Gal. 6:7–9).

Prayer

FIRST THINGS FIRST

A leader once encountered a huge task. He was confronted by overwhelming problems, including short deadlines, insufficient staff, tight budgets, personal attacks, external opposition and internal conflicts. How did he begin?

When I heard these things, I sat down and wept. For some days I mourned and fasted and prayed before the God of heaven. Then I said: "LORD, the God of heaven, the great and awesome God, who keeps his covenant of love with those who love him and keep his commandments, let your ear be attentive and your eyes open to hear the prayer your servant is praying before you day and night for your servants, the people of Israel. I confess the sins we Israelites, including myself and my father's family, have committed against you. We have acted very wickedly toward you. We have not obeyed the commands, decrees and laws you gave your servant Moses. Remember the instruction you gave your servant Moses, saying, 'If you are unfaithful, I will scatter you among the nations, but if you return to me and obey my commands, then even if your exiled people are at the farthest horizon, I will gather them from there and bring them to the place I have chosen as a dwelling for my Name.'

"They are your servants and your people, whom you redeemed by your great strength and your mighty hand. O Lord, let your ear be attentive to the prayer of this your servant and to the prayer of your servants who delight in revering your name. Give your servant success today by granting him favor in the presence of this man." I was cupbearer to the king. (Neh. 1:4–11)

What was the task facing Nehemiah? To completely rebuild the destroyed city of Jerusalem. Chuck Swindoll and John White have written excellent books presenting the king's cupbearer as another excellent model for leadership. As they emphasize, Nehemiah's first step was to sit down...and pray.

A CHANGE OF HEART

As Andrew prepared for a major strategic planning session, he sensed that management was not willing to face the truth. Nor would it be willing to make the changes necessary to align the company with market realities. In the past, he would have forced his way through the situation and then been angry over the certain lack of a satisfactory response.

This time, Andrew sought God in prayer and asked him to provide leadership. God led him to John 8:32: "Then you will know the truth, and the truth will set you free." He received the verse as a promise. He also continued to pray for God to soften all hearts so truth could be received and decisions would be made based on what was revealed. God answered his prayer as management responded by hearing and accepting the truth.

The company was realigned, moving onto a path of success. More important, the leaders' hearts continued to soften, just as Andrew's heart had in turning to God through prayer rather than reverting to his old way. Together they became increasingly able to receive the truth of the gospel and consistently willing to walk with God.

Patience

"So let my lord go on ahead of his servant, while I move along slowly at the pace of the flocks and herds before me and the pace of the children, until I come to my lord in Seir." (Gen. 33:14)

A person's wisdom yields patience; it is to one's glory to overlook an offense. (Prov. 19:11)

Be patient with everyone. (1 Thess. 5:14)

PROTECTION: "'I will place shepherds over them who will tend them, and they will no longer be afraid or terrified, nor will any be missing,' declares the LORD" (Jer. 23:4).

The Lord Is My Shepherd

He makes me lie down in green pastures,
he leads me beside quiet waters. (Ps. 23:2)

PEACE: "[Whoever would love life and see good days] must seek peace and pursue it" (1 Pet. 3:11).

The Lord Is My Shepherd

For you are with me. (Ps. 23:4)

Provision

The Lord Is My Shepherd

The LORD is my shepherd, I shall not be in want...my cup overflows. (Ps. 23:1, 5)

Command those who are rich in this present world not to be arrogant nor to put their hope in wealth, which is so uncertain, but to put their hope in God, who richly provides us with everything for our enjoyment. (1 Tim. 6:17)

Anyone who does not provide for their relatives, and especially for their own household, has denied the faith and is worse than an unbeliever. (1 Tim. 5:8).

Leadership Insight

When faced with difficulty and uncertainty, God calls us to persevere. Not to give up but to seek him and thus, in prayer, to ask, seek, knock. Look for his pathway, look for his discernment—what is going on at the heart level? How does God desire to affect our character and walk as shepherd leaders? Thus we expect him to give power for what lies ahead, a sense of his presence (in other words, something larger is going on here) and provision for the business.

> Consider it pure joy, my brothers and sisters, whenever you face trials of many kinds, because you know that the testing of your faith produces perseverance. Let perseverance finish its work so that you may be mature and complete, not lacking anything. If any of you lacks wisdom, you should ask God, who gives generously to all without finding fault, and it will be given to you. (James 1:2–5)

SHEPHERD

Healing

> Therefore confess your sins to each other and pray for each other so that you may be healed. (James 5:16)

TO HELP AND TO HEAL

The employee who needed heart surgery, Carl, was expected to recover in routine fashion and return to work. I assumed that my response to the dilemma originally presented by his situation fulfilled my responsibility as a shepherd. I was wrong.

Late one night after Carl's operation, the telephone rang. His wife called to say that his condition unexpectedly took a turn for the worse. Rather than seek the hospital chaplain or a church pastor, she contacted me, not knowing where else to turn. I, too, was at a loss. The phone line fell quiet.

Silently praying, "Now what, Lord?" I was instantly convicted to help—to visit Carl and keep his wife company. I took a simple wooden cross along just in case I also needed comfort.

Two of Carl's colleagues, high schoolers who worked part-time with him in the warehouse, were already in the hospital waiting room. They were praying and reading their Bibles. Since the thought of bringing my Bible hadn't occurred to me, it was a humbling sight.

In the intensive care unit, Carl was comatose and still hemorrhaging. Standing awkwardly by Carl's bed, it finally dawned on me to pray as well. With his wife's hand in mine, and the cross in my other hand clasped over his, we prayed, simply asking the Lord to help and heal Carl. Meanwhile, a nurse entered to adjust some equipment. Annoyed by the distraction, we were about to ask her to leave when she suddenly looked up from the monitor. With disbelief on her face, she exclaimed, "The hemorrhage has stopped!"

Within a couple of weeks, Carl was back to work. After remaining with the company for several years, he eventually left for more schooling. Carl answered a call to the formal study of how to feed and nourish—as a chef.

A THOROUGHLY MODERN MIRACLE

His brother faced what was scheduled to be a ninety-minute surgery to remove cancer threatening the right eye. Four and a half hours into the procedure, a physician called him to verify permission to remove the eye. Even if left in place, it would almost certainly be completely useless because all of the supporting muscles had been removed.

He was confused by the call. His brother had previously consented to removal if it became necessary. It only took two minutes or so, but the conversation seemed to last an eternity. The decision was made to leave it in, if only for cosmetic and psychological reasons. With no support structure in place, the medical team placed six feet of gauze packing into the cavity behind the eye and completed the operation.

Even though the optic nerve and blood vessels were left largely intact, the odds were stacked against his brother ever being able to use the eye again. At least it was in place for the time being. His brother could decide for himself to remove it when the inevitable collapse into the socket occurred. For now, he asked the Holy Spirit to heal his brother and fill the void behind the eye with love. Others joined in prayer.

Later, after the external bandage was removed, the doctor began the nearly weeklong process of extracting one foot of packing every day. Each day, he expected the eye to weaken and fall back. Each day, people continued to pray.

On the sixth day, the final foot of gauze was removed. Nothing happened. After carefully examining his brother's eye, the doctor and hospital staff had no explanation.

After two weeks, a neuro-ophthalmologist was called in to make an examination. He candidly suggested that he apply physical pressure to the eye so he might be present when removal became necessary. He pushed. And pushed. Still, nothing happened. Finally, the specialist said, "I don't know what the surgeon thought he did, but the support structure is as strong as the good eye."

> This salvation, which was first announced by the Lord, was confirmed to us by those who heard him. God also testified to it by signs, wonders and various miracles. (Heb. 2:3-4)

Hearing

WE HEAR GOD

> "Whoever has ears, let them hear." (Matt. 11:15)

> "My sheep listen to my voice; I know them, and they follow me." (John 10:27)

> "Whoever belongs to God hears what God says. The reason you do not hear is that you do not belong to God." (John 8:47)

> "Very truly I tell you, whoever hears my word and believes him who sent me has eternal life and will not be judged but has crossed over from death to life." (John 5:24)

WE HEAR ONE ANOTHER

> Everyone should be quick to listen, slow to speak and slow to become angry. (James 1:19)

> The wise listen to advice. (Prov. 12:15)

> The words of the wise are like goads, their collected sayings like firmly embedded nails—given by one shepherd. (Eccl. 12:11)

GOD HEARS US

> This is the confidence we have in approaching God: that if we ask anything according to his will, he hears us. And if we know that he hears us—whatever we ask—we know that we have what we asked of him. (1 John 5:14-15)

HEAR, HEAR

Andrew and his group called on a company for months with little response. Repeated inquiries and careful preparations began to feel like a waste of time. An important project unfortunately seemed destined not to happen.

Yet, having learned that God's view of things is often not ours, they asked the Father again, "What should we do?"

Turning to quiet meditation and prayer, Andrew heard back. "Bypass who you are talking to and go straight to the chief financial officer with your story. He needs your service."

Having heard, they made another call. The CFO welcomed them, allowing them to present their wares. Ultimately Andrew's group was selected to provide service. Later, after they performed with excellence, even people who were initially resentful toward them responded with praise and thanksgiving.

Heeding

Whoever heeds correction is honored (Prov. 13:18), shows prudence (Prov. 15:5) and gains understanding (Prov. 15:32).

HELP: "Suppose one of you has a hundred sheep and loses one of them. Doesn't he leave the ninety-nine in the open country and go after the lost sheep until he finds it? And when he finds it, he joyfully puts it on his shoulders and goes home. Then he calls his friends and neighbors together and says, 'Rejoice with me; I have found my lost sheep'" (Luke 15:4–6).

HEART: "Then I will give you shepherds after my own heart, who will lead you with knowledge and understanding" (Jer. 3:15).

Leadership Insight

A shepherd cares about those who are wounded. He does not discard them but seeks them out and asks God the Father for redemptive healing and restoration, whether needs lie in physical, emotional or spiritual realms. We are to seek with a sense of expectancy and to keep asking at deeper levels than business finances and functions, desiring that God reveal and fulfill his redemptive purposes. A willingness to seek God's wisdom and an expectation that he will

answer are important leadership characteristics. God wants to speak his will and expects us to follow when he does.

> If any of you lacks wisdom, you should ask God, who gives generously to all without finding fault, and it will be given to you. But when you ask, you must believe and not doubt, because the one who doubts is like a wave of the sea, blown and tossed by the wind. That person should not expect to receive anything from the Lord. Such a person is double-minded and unstable in all they do. (James 1:5–8)

SHEPHERD

Encouragement

Courage is a matter of the heart. Literally, the word is derived from the French word for heart, *coeur*. As leaders, we can do one of two things. We can put courage in the hearts of our people—to encourage. Or, we can take courage out of the hearts of our people—to discourage. Which will it be?

> We have different gifts, according to the grace given to each of us. If your gift is...to encourage, then give encouragement. (Rom. 12:6-8)

> Therefore encourage each other with these words...Encourage one another and build each other up, just as in fact you are doing. (1 Thess. 4:18; 5:11)

> Be prepared in season and out of season; correct, rebuke and encourage—with great patience and careful instruction. (2 Tim. 4:2)

> Encourage the young men to be self-controlled. (Titus 2:6)

> But encourage one another daily, as long as it is called "Today," so that none of you may be hardened by sin's deceitfulness. (Heb. 3:13)

> Not giving up meeting together, as some are in the habit of doing, but encouraging one another—and all the more as you see the Day approaching. (Heb. 10:25)

TO ENCOURAGE AND ENDURE

Luke was scheduled to fly to New York City on Tuesday for a visit with his mother. When he awoke that morning, something was troubling him. Despite how much he truly enjoyed traveling, he had butterflies in his stomach, a feeling he hadn't experienced for many years. It was September 11, 2001.

Luke calmed down after completing his daily devotions. He turned on the television. At the moment he glanced at the screen, a large passenger airplane hit the south tower of the World Trade Center. It seemed like a movie, too surreal to really be happening. The sense of shock was instantaneous. Yet somehow an inexplicable sense of calmness quickly followed. He called his office, where everyone was understandably dazed and scared. When the towers soon collapsed, he knew in his heart it was a time to set an example of encouragement and endurance through adversity.

Knowing he needed to do something, he opened a Bible to search for words of comfort. He always found help in Scripture, and it seemed like an opportunity to share with others. Any thought of offending someone was lost in the circumstance of dire emotional needs. If one person found solace, it would be worth it. With verses in hand, Luke went to his office, where he spent time comforting others one by one and sharing Scripture when so moved.

Luke also sensed a larger need. Feeling limited by the physical inability to talk personally with each of several hundred employees, he sent out an email titled "Words of Faith and Encouragement." The response was immediate as people responded by sharing their own private concerns.

Later in the week, President Bush called for a moment of silence and prayer. People at Luke's office gathered in the company parking lot and formed a circle. It was a special time, with many openly praying and sharing their concerns. The circle included people of all faiths—Christian, Hindu, Jew and Muslim.

As Luke scanned the participants, he noticed a young woman wearing a veil. She was Islamic, and she stood with head bowed. As his eyes settled on her, she looked up at him. He stepped toward her with his arms opened. She responded in kind. In the middle of the parking lot, amidst a hundred people, Luke, a Christian, and Modi, a Muslim, embraced. Both felt the pain of tragedy while realizing the need for healing.

In the ensuing months Luke, as chief executive officer, periodically shared additional words of faith and encouragement via company-wide email. It remains an ongoing tradition.

For everything that was written in the past was written to teach us, so that through the endurance taught in the Scriptures and the encouragement they provide we might have hope. May the God who gives endurance and encouragement give you the same attitude of mind toward each other that Christ Jesus had, so that with one mind and one voice you may glorify the God and Father of our Lord Jesus Christ. (Rom. 15:4–6)

Endurance

If we are distressed, it is for your comfort and salvation; if we are comforted, it is for your comfort, which produces in you patient endurance of the same sufferings we suffer. (2 Cor. 1:6)

[Be] strengthened with all power according to his glorious might so that you may have great endurance and patience. (Col. 1:11)

Pursue righteousness, godliness, faith, love, endurance and gentleness. (1 Tim. 6:11)

Join with me in suffering, like a good soldier of Christ Jesus. (2 Tim. 2:3)

If we endure, we will also reign with him. (2 Tim. 2:12)

Endure hardship as discipline; God is treating you as his children. For what children are not disciplined by their father? (Heb. 12:7)

Leadership Insight

While providing an environment of hope, we will need to walk day by day in places where God is asking us to provide a word of encouragement. A single statement offered after listening carefully may prove pivotal in helping a colleague get past an obstacle.

We are then to stand with endurance and demonstrate how, together, we can get through any roadblock. Not because we try harder but because we seek the One who can get us through and provide us with strength to endure.

SHEPHERD

Respect

RESPECTFULLY YOURS

Luke, the CEO, continues to share occasional "Words of Faith and Encouragement" via emails to everyone at his company. Sometimes the occasion is an important holiday season; other times it simply follows a unique personal prompting. In every instance, he is committed to sensitivity and governed by the desire to remain respectful to people of all faiths. Here are a few examples.

APRIL 10, 2003

I recently came across a poem written by John Wesley, an eighteenth century teacher and pastor. It summarizes a philosophy of life that respects humanity and an individual's responsibility to make this a better and safer world for all people.

> Do all the good you can,
> By all the means you can,
> In all the ways you can,
> In all the places you can,
> At all the times you can,
> To all the people you can,
> As long as you ever can.

Let us commit to helping each other by sharing each other's burdens in times of need, encouraging each other, and doing good in all things.

APRIL 18, 2003

As we begin this Easter weekend, I would like to share some thoughts that are meaningful to me. One of the attributes making our company a special and unique workplace is the respect we have for all people. While you know my personal beliefs, you also know we respect each person's right to their own faith.

For people who celebrate Easter, which is the death and resurrection of Jesus Christ, it is a time of joy. It also represents a time of sacrifice, compassion, forgiveness, and a new future. It means letting go of past hurts and wounds and believing that Jesus, through his death on the cross, put sin to death as well. And when Jesus was resurrected (brought back to life from death), he offered us an opportunity through faith to receive his complete forgiveness and have a new beginning in life. Once we accept his forgiveness, we then have the ability to forgive and reconcile with those who have wronged or hurt us.

Perhaps this Easter season, we can take this special time and forgive others just like we have been forgiven. Maybe we will experience healing of broken or strained relationships. What joy it would bring to those around us—family, friends, and even co-workers.

Whatever your beliefs, may you experience a weekend of joy and forgiveness. I personally want to express my appreciation for your hard work as part of our company family and wish you a Happy and Joyous Easter celebration.

DECEMBER 24, 2003

As we begin our celebration of the holidays, I would like to share some personal thoughts with you. I believe the season is an opportunity for people of all faiths and walks of life to take some time to fellowship with family and friends, share a meal, exchange gifts, do a good deed for another, or simply tell someone you love them and appreciate all they have done for you. In essence, it is a time to forget our differences and celebrate a common bond of mercy, compassion, and love.

For those of us of the Christian faith, the holiday season is a celebration of the birth of Jesus Christ, who Christians believe is the Son of God, the Messiah. The Bible says that "God is love" (1 John 4:8), and Jesus as his Son also represents love.

In a recent sermon, a pastor described a dual meaning for Christmas that may be relevant to many of us. While the day represents the physical birth of Jesus for Christians, it can also give others the opportunity to celebrate the birth of love in our hearts. The holiday season gives each of us an annual opportunity to recommit to care for each other and, in love, to serve one another.

My blessings to you and your family for a Happy Holiday Season, Merry Christmas, and a Joyous New Year.

Show proper respect to everyone. (1 Pet. 2:17)

Honor the LORD with your wealth. (Prov. 3:9)

Reconciliation

"In your anger do not sin": Do not let the sun go down while you are still angry, and do not give the devil a foothold. (Eph. 4:26–27)

"Therefore, if you are offering your gift at the altar and there remember that your brother or sister has something against you, leave your gift there in front of the altar. First go and be reconciled to them; then come and offer your gift." (Matt. 5:23–24)

The Lord Is My Shepherd

You prepare a table before me in the presence of my enemies. (Ps. 23:5)

RESTORATION: "The land by the sea will become pastures having wells for shepherds and pens for flocks...there they will find pasture. In the evening they will lie down...The LORD their God will care for them; he will restore their fortunes" (Zeph. 2:6-7).

The Lord Is My Shepherd

He refreshes my soul. (Ps. 23:3)

SOME SORELY NEEDED R&R

Andrew continually struggled with an executive who was annoyingly egotistical and frequently self-serving. The executive was competent but hardly a team player and not at all helpful for group dynamics and decision-making. Andrew's first thought was to terminate and replace him.

As a shepherd leader, though, his first thought was renewed. He chose instead to seek a full measure of reconciliation and restoration. As he prayed, he realized that the executive was in bondage, trapped with a profound sense of insecurity. Andrew then took him out to lunch to talk on a personal level about his life and struggles. The executive opened up, sharing about captivating fear and worry.

Andrew asked if he would be interested in seeking God's Word and finding out what God had to say about fears and worries. He was, and he is now being transformed in the process—reconciled at the personal level and restored to becoming a valuable member of the executive team.

REWARDS: "Then your Father, who sees what is done in secret, will reward you" (Matt. 6:4).

Righteousness

For in the gospel the righteousness from God is revealed—a righteousness that is by faith from first to last, just as it is written: "The righteous will live by faith." (Rom. 1:17)

The righteous cry out, and the LORD hears them; he delivers them from all their troubles. (Ps. 34:17)

THE SHEPHERD AND HIS STAFF

The Lord Is My Shepherd

He guides me along the right paths for his name's sake. (Ps. 23:3)

Leadership Insight

Part of our character as leaders is that we live with respect, always with an eye to reconciliation and restoration. "All this is from God, who reconciled us to himself through Christ and gave us the ministry of reconciliation" (2 Cor. 5:18).

Instead of our first inclination—superficial disappointment and ultimate rejection—we are called to go deeper. We are to seek understanding of struggles at personal and spiritual levels. By offering reconciliation and restoration, we allow God to do his work of redemption, of having his children come to expect and receive the fullness of salvation and wholeness of being.

SHEPHERD

Decision and Discipline

How does a leader make the right decision in the right way, without procrastinating or becoming paralyzed? Here's an E-A-S-Y framework based on biblical values.

E: Entrust the decision to God.
"Come to me all you who are weary and burdened, and I will give you rest. Take my yoke upon you and learn from me, for I am gentle and humble in heart, and you will find rest for your souls. For my yoke is easy and my burden is light." (Matt. 11:28-30)

A: Acknowledge that God is in control.
But our citizenship is in heaven. And we eagerly await a Savior from there, the Lord Jesus Christ, who, by the power that enables him to bring everything under his control, will transform our lowly bodies so that they will be like his glorious body. (Phil. 3:20–21)

S: Seek God's guidance.
I instruct you in the way of wisdom and lead you along straight paths. (Prov. 4:11)

Y: Yield to God's will.
"Now then," said Joshua, "throw away the foreign gods that are among you and yield your hearts to the LORD, the God of Israel." (Josh. 24:23)

How does one go about discerning God's will in order to yield to it? Several years ago, a lay pastor at a local church shared a framework that continues to help me.

G: Go to the source.

"First seek the counsel of the LORD." (1 Kings 22:5)

"Acknowledge the God of your father, and serve him with wholehearted devotion and with a willing mind, for the LORD searches every heart and understands every desire and every thought. If you seek him, he will be found by you." (1 Chron. 28:9)

O: Obtain guidance.

Let the wise listen and add to their learning, and let the discerning get guidance. (Prov. 1:5)

D: Declare a commitment to obey God's Word.

It is the LORD your God you must follow, and him you must revere. Keep his commands and obey him; serve him and hold fast to him. (Deut. 13:4)

S: Stillness in prayer.

"Be still, and know that I am God." (Ps. 46:10)

W: Wisdom from other believers.

Wisdom is found in those who take advice. (Prov. 13:10)

I: Invite them to meet in counsel.

Walk with the wise and become wise. (Prov. 13:20)

L: Learn from them.

Plans fail for lack of counsel, but with many advisers they succeed. (Prov. 15:22)

L: Listen to them.

Whoever heeds life-giving correction will be at home among the wise. (Prov. 15:31)

Discipline

Leaders should exercise discipline in their walk. "God disciplines us for our good, in order that we may share in his holiness" (Heb. 12:10).

STATIONS ON THE ROAD TO FREEDOM

If you set out to seek freedom, then learn above all things to govern your soul and your senses, for fear that your passions and longing may lead you away from the path you should follow. Chaste be your mind and your body, and both in subjection, obediently, steadfastly seeking the aim set before them; only through discipline may a man learn to be free.

Discipline proved to be a great adventure for the author of these words. Along the way, he

- Emerged from a loving secular home to become a Christian pastor
- Wrote more than a dozen books
- Lived in Barcelona, New York, London and Berlin
- Traveled to Africa, Cuba, Mexico, Rome and throughout Europe
- Spearheaded an international ecumenical movement
- Started a "confessing" church when his denomination sold out to dictatorial influence
- Established underground communities after being relegated to virtual exile
- Smuggled Jews out of Germany to safety
- Participated in an assassination conspiracy
- Was betrothed to a woman he was never able to marry
- Was arrested and imprisoned
- And, ultimately, paid the full cost of discipleship

Dietrich Bonhoeffer was thirty-nine years old when he was hanged under direct orders from Hitler, just three weeks before Berlin fell to American and Allied forces. "Discipline," as well as other stations on the road to freedom, was written a few months earlier in correspondence from Bonhoeffer to Eberhard Bethge, his best friend. It appears in the Christian classic Bonhoeffer's *Letters and Papers From Prison.*

DILIGENCE: "The plans of the diligent lead to profit as surely as haste leads to poverty" (Prov. 21:5).

DO THE WORD OF GOD: "Do not merely listen to the word, and so deceive yourselves. Do what it says" (James 1:22).

DO NOT BE DECEITFUL: "Therefore, rid yourselves of all malice and all deceit, hypocrisy, envy, and slander of every kind" (1 Pet. 2:1).

DO NOT BE DOWNCAST: "Why, my soul, are you downcast? Why so disturbed within me? Put your hope in God, for I will yet praise him, my Savior and my God" (Ps. 42:5, 11). (A "cast" sheep, or a sheep "cast down," is an old English term for a sheep turned over on its back and unable to get up by itself.)

DO NOT WORRY: "Do not be anxious about anything, but in every situation, by prayer and petition, with thanksgiving, present your requests to God" (Phil. 4:6).

THE FOREMAN

The company stored certain products in an out-of-town warehouse. Several years ago, product package inserts needed to be replaced with a new, easier-to-use version. The changeover would involve opening 4,000 boxes. Stan, the responsible executive, was eager to fly home the same night. He wanted the work done in a single day.

A group of ten day laborers was hired to tackle the job. As an incentive, Stan guaranteed them a full day's pay. He also promised to provide lunch if everything could be completed by midday.

The group organized itself into two teams, established work rules and started in on the task. Though everything seemed to be going smoothly, Stan wanted to identify their leader. With everyone's attention, he asked, "Who's your supervisor?"

Not missing a beat, a man to his right replied, "Jesus Christ is our foreman." Their love for God put Stan to shame.

Without knowing whether or not they would have work assigned by their temporary agency the next day, the workers happily and whole-heartedly completed a tedious job in four hours. As they enjoyed lunch together with smiles on their faces, Stan was confronted in a profound way with the pettiness of his concern about his own ability to return home later that day. What a beautiful illustration of biblical truth.

"Therefore do not worry about tomorrow, for tomorrow will worry about itself. Each day has enough trouble of its own." (Matt. 6:34)

Leadership Insight

Our decisions are intended to be God's decisions—his wisdom, his view, his leading, his pathway. Instead of relying solely on human analysis and trying to figure out anything and everything on our own, we are to seek him, following a process that allows God to operate. By seeking him daily, we come to expect his revealed will, follow his way, and grow as participants in his ultimate leadership program—as shepherd leaders.

"But seek first his kingdom and his righteousness, and all these things will be given to you as well." (Matt. 6:33)

In the end, there are two kinds of shepherds: on one hand, shepherds who take care of their flock; on the other hand, shepherds who only take care of themselves. My prayer is that you will answer the call of Jesus, the ultimate role model for leadership, and be transformed into a shepherd after his own image. Amen.

Reflection: The Piney River Flock

It was mid-August 2003. Beneath crystal-clear blue skies, I hiked alone along the remote reaches of the Piney River Trail in Colorado. The smell of pine from large evergreens mixed with the scent of small wildflowers to fill the chilly air. With wind whistling through the trees and water babbling over the rocks, there was no sound or sign of civilization.

Suddenly, I heard a single "baa-a-a" in the distance. I stopped in my tracks, not knowing the source. Then I heard more of the same. Following the sounds, I eventually reached an area where a clearing was visible across the river. There was movement on the opposite bank. A solitary black sheep appeared. Several other sheep soon followed. The black sheep led them to the edge of the water. After drinking, they moved into the shade of nearby trees, where they lay down to rest. What a wonderful sight! A sense of God's peace descended as I paused to watch.

Later that day, when I described the glorious scene to my wife, she turned my attention to Psalm 23. The psalm served as a poignant culmination of my experience with the Piney River flock. It also reinforced the importance of the shepherding message in my life and relationships with others. The always familiar yet still fresh words are an enduring reminder of the One who lovingly shepherds us while he longingly seeks to develop us as shepherds.

PSALM 23

A psalm of David. The LORD is my shepherd, I lack nothing. He makes me lie down in green pastures, he leads me beside quiet waters, he refreshes my soul. He guides me along the right paths for his name's sake. Even though I walk through the darkest valley, I will fear no evil, for you are with me; your rod and your staff, they comfort me. You prepare a table before me in the presence of my enemies. You anoint my head with oil; my cup overflows. Surely your goodness and love will follow me all the days of my life, and I will dwell in the house of the LORD forever.

The Great Shepherd

May the God of peace, who through the blood of the eternal covenant brought back from the dead our Lord Jesus, that great Shepherd of the sheep, equip you with everything good for doing his will, and may he work in us what is pleasing to him, through Jesus Christ, to whom be glory forever and ever. Amen. (Heb. 13:20-21)

Afterword

"Take care of the troops," my father would say. When I was a child, he often told stories and shared pictures of his service in World War II. Afterward, he'd close each tale in the same way. The heartfelt moral of the story was always to "take care of the troops." His words of wisdom helped forge within me a lifelong interest in a certain brand of leadership.

My passion for leadership started early. While growing up, I read countless books about great leaders. Among them were the Landmark Books published by Random House beginning in 1952. The best authors of the day were commissioned to write about important historical figures and topics. The series came to encompass well over 100 action-packed narratives with wonderful biographical detail.

I read them all. Favorites included stories of leaders like Dwight D. Eisenhower and innovators like Robert Fulton. Books captured my imagination and motivated me to learn about history through the lives and experiences of the subjects.

Of course, my father and his stories had the most lasting influence. By the time of America's involvement in the war, he had graduated from college and was accepted to the United States Army's Officer Candidate School, the most ambitious and comprehensive leadership-training program ever undertaken. The regular army had several hundred officers during the summer of 1939. At its peak strength in 1945, the number had grown by tens of thousands.

My father's experience, however, was not all guts and glory. Instead, he served behind the lines in a support function. His job, and that of his troops, was to set up bakeries to make bread. American troops had to eat, and my father fed them whenever and wherever they were hungry.

Few of us ever consider the support functions and planning required to recruit, train and lead an army. Without soldiers in support of those serving on the front lines, forward progress would grind to a halt. For example, the lightning-fast advance of the U.S. Army Tank Corps across France and into Germany would have faltered without supplies of essential materiel, including fuel, ammunition and food.

As a result, each of my father's stories ended with the same encouragement. Commitment to the troops was completely engrained in his character. A child obviously has no troops of his own, but I never forgot those words. Even while reading about great leaders, I constantly sought evidence to show that they took care of their troops. They did.

A wonderful lesson in life was planted deep within my head and heart. My father was a quiet, rather introverted person who cared not for fame or fortune. He always thought first of his troops. As a leader, he fed them bread, a humble service to his men. As a father, he nourished me as well with his words and a great lesson in life. In the end, my inheritance was not material things. Instead, my father's simple and profound words "Take care of the troops" became a priceless legacy with life-changing impact.

My father passed away in 1982. At that time, I was living in a foreign country, and by the time I returned for his funeral all the arrangements had been made by other family members. Several years later, as I was looking through some files, I found a small scrap of paper. It was so small, I almost threw it away. However, scribbled on the paper was a note from my father. It simply said, "Bury me at Arlington." When I asked my mother, she recalled a conversation she had with my father about Arlington, but in the midst of her mourning she had forgotten about it.

As time went on my mother and I often discussed moving my father to Arlington National Cemetery, but there was always a reason that it could not be done. Just before my mother passed away in 2010, a relative told me that my mother had initiated inquiries about how to move my father to Arlington. I told my mother that I would handle it.

After my mother passed away, I began the process. Finally, in June 2011, my father was moved to Arlington National Cemetery. As a World War II veteran and officer, he received full military honors—a band, six body bearers, a bugler, an escort and a firing party. My father took care of his troops, and in the end his troops honored him and took care of him by gently and reverently placing him in his final resting place along with his troops, the troops he never forgot or left behind.

Over the years, in a variety of life and business settings, a question arose. What does it truly mean for a leader to take care of the troops? When I was grown to manhood and finally ready, the answer, in Jesus' words, began to come alive.

> When they had finished eating, Jesus said to Simon Peter, "Simon son of John, do you love me more than these?" "Yes, Lord," he said, "you know that I love you." Jesus said, "Feed my lambs." Again Jesus said, "Simon son of John, do you love me?" He answered, "Yes, Lord, you know that I love you." Jesus said, "Take care of my sheep." The third time he said to him, "Simon son of John, do you love me?" Peter was hurt because Jesus asked him the third time, "Do you love me?" He said, "Lord, you know all things; you know that I love you." Jesus said, "Feed my sheep." (John 21:15-17)

A Shepherd's Calling

It was a mid-November night, and I was in the midst of work on this book. As I pondered the role of a shepherd, words began to flood my thoughts. Not wanting to forget, I hurriedly recorded the words. If you are called to be a shepherd, I hope this simple prayer will serve as a regular reminder of your eternal legacy from God the Father and Jesus Christ his Son.

I AM CALLED TO BE A SHEPHERD

I am the Lord's shepherd
Saved by his Son
Surrendered to his will.
He is my Savior
Giving me strength through his Spirit
That I may selflessly serve his flock.
I shall be a faithful steward sharing with others.
Hearing his Word, I will give hope for a bright future.
I am an example to his flock
Exalting his name and encouraging others.
I pray patiently for his peace and will protect his flock.
I will be humble, heeding his calling.
With empathy and endurance, I will be a righteous shepherd
Repenting of my sins, renewing my mind
Restoring glory to his name, reconciling one to another.
I will be a doer of his Word, discerning his will
And dedicating my life to loving him and his flock.
Amen.

Acknowledgments

Jesus is the author and perfecter of our faith. He's also the inspiration for this work. *The Shepherd and His Staff* came as a progressive revelation over the past two decades. Whether roadside or at 40,000 feet in the air—on the ground or somewhere over North America, South America, Europe, Africa or Asia—I've simply tried to listen and obey wherever and whenever the Holy Spirit has offered God's gifts of grace.

As the message of this book was formulating in my head and heart, I was blessed to meet Rich, a business consultant and pastor who formerly served as senior vice president for a Fortune 500 company. He has faithfully walked with me in this journey as my executive coach and accountability partner, advising and counseling me across a range of business, spiritual and personal matters. His general wisdom and insights and example of faith in the workplace are invaluable; his specific contributions to this work were indispensable. To Rich goes my profound gratitude.

Over 25 years ago I served as a mentor—a shepherd—for a young professional. Through God's creative providence, our respective pilgrimages recently reunited us. Thank you to Tom, who helped me pull the pieces together, uncovered the original Peter Principle, and found the words for this work.

The Lord also called Sarah, a talented young artist, to add visual depth and expression to this work.

Blessings and honor to the other men and women I've had the privilege of working with over the years. I'm grateful for their patience and forgiveness when I've missed the mark as a leader. I'm also delighted by the countless instances when they've responded to a call to lead and be like a shepherd with courage, maturity and faith.

David is the man who showed me the Way in 1981. He continues to help keep me focused on biblical truths, not allowing me to run adrift.

Ken and Phil acted on inspiration to found the Center for FaithWalk Leadership, and I'm grateful to them for establishing the Lead Like Jesus movement.

On the home front, my hope is for my children to continue seeking and finding nourishment from the good Shepherd. I also pray they may experience the impact of my father's true legacy as they grow to become leaders in their own lives.

Finally, my beloved wife has been a godsend every step along the path of our lives together. From before the days of business and personal dilemmas and decisions to the pastoral beauty and symbolism of the Piney River trip and beyond, she has faithfully and lovingly pointed me to the great Shepherd. To her goes my abiding love and gratitude.

For More Information

Just as I was enlightened and inspired by books and their authors while growing up, the written and spoken words of others were an immense benefit during the time *The Shepherd and His Staff* was received as a progressive revelation. First and foremost stands God's Word as revealed in the Bible and shared by the Holy Spirit throughout this pilgrimage. In addition, as this message was formulating in my head and heart, I was consciously guided and undoubtedly otherwise influenced by the contributions of many who share a vital interest in leadership.

I am especially grateful for the wisdom and writings of Ken Blanchard, Phil Hodges, Henry Blackaby, and Gene Wilkes, among others to whom I'm also indebted. A selected list of good books encountered along the way follows.

Henry Blackaby and Richard Blackaby
Spiritual Leadership: Moving People on to God's Agenda

Ken Blanchard
The Heart of A Leader: Insight of the Art of Influence
We Are the Beloved: A Spiritual Journey

Ken Blanchard and Phil Hodges
The Servant Leader: Transforming Your Heart, Head, Hands & Habits

Ken Blanchard, Bill Hybels, and Phil Hodges
Leadership by the Book: Tools to Transform Your Workplace

Lee G. Bolman and Terrence E. Deal
Leading with Soul: An Uncommon Journey of Spirit

Bob Buford
Game Plan: Winning Strategies for the Second Half of Your Life
Half Time: Changing Your Game Plan from Success to Significance

Michael Cardone Sr.
Never Too Late For A New Beginning

Melissa Giovagnoli
Angels in the Workplace: Stories and Inspirations for Creating a New World of Work

Dwight L. Johnson
The Transparent Leader: Spiritual Secrets of Nineteen Successful Men

Laurie Beth Jones
The Path: Creating Your Mission Statement for Work and for Life

Larry S. Julian
God Is My CEO: Following God's Principles in a Bottom-Line World

Kevin Leman and William Pentak
The Way of the Shepherd: 7 Ancient Secrets to Managing Productive People

Charles C. Manz
The Leadership Wisdom of Jesus: Practical Lessons for Today

Rich Marshall
God at Work: Discovering the Anointing for Business

Tom Marshall
Understanding Leadership: Fresh Perspectives on the Essentials of New Testament Leadership

Kevin W. McCarthy
The On-Purpose Business: Doing More of What You Do Best More Profitably

Blaine McCormick and David Davenport
Shepherd Leadership: Wisdom for Leaders from Psalm 23

Michael Novak
Business as a Calling: Work and the Examined Life

William C. Pollard
The Soul of the Firm

Doug Sherman and William Hendricks
How to Balance Competing Time Demands: Keeping the Five Most Important Areas of Your Life in Perspective

Ed Silvoso
Anointed for Business: How Christians Can Use Their Influence in the Marketplace to Change the World

David L. Steward
Doing Business by the Good Book: 52 Lessons on Success Straight from the Bible

Rick Warren
The Purpose-Driven Life: What On Earth Am I Here For?

C. Gene Wilkes
Jesus on Leadership: Discovering the Secrets of Servant Leadership from the Life of Christ

Ultimate acknowledgment and praise once again go to Jesus, the author of all that is worthwhile in this work.

If you would like to contact Theodore Mistra, please write to him in care of
Castle Quay Books
4450 Danielson Drive, Lake Worth, Florida, 33467

About the Author

Theodore Mistra is retired chairman of the board and chief executive officer for a life sciences company with hundreds of employees and approximately a hundred million dollars in sales. He is the graduate of an Ivy League business school. Ted and his wife are the parents of three children.

Theodore Mistra is a pen name for two reasons. When praying about the message of this book, Theodore and his wife were convicted by the Holy Spirit that it was to be a testimony about the LORD and not about them. The Good Shepherd was to receive all the glory and attention; Theodore was just a messenger. Second, the stories and anecdotes are true and were shared in confidence. Thus to protect the privacy of those individuals Theodore used a pen name and changed the real names of the persons described in the book. Theodore and his wife pray that the reader will understand the sincerity of their decision.

Do you need a speaker?

Do you want Theodore Mistra to speak to your group or event? Then contact Larry Willard by phone at (416) 573-3249 or email larrywillard@rogers.com.

Whether you want to purchase bulk copies of *The Shepherd and His Staff* or buy another book for a friend, get it now online at **www.castlequaybooksbooks.com.**